I want to be a Mechanic

I WANT TO BE A
Mechanic

DAN LIEBMAN

FIREFLY BOOKS

A FIREFLY BOOK

Published by Firefly Books Ltd. 2003

Copyright © 2003 Firefly Books Ltd.

First Printing 2003

Publisher Cataloging-in-Publication Data (U.S.) (Library of Congress Standards)

Liebman, Dan.
  I want to be a mechanic / Dan Liebman.—1st ed.
[24] p. : col. photos. ;   cm. – (I want to be)
Summary: Photographs and easy-to-read text describe the job of a mechanic.
ISBN 1-55297-695-5
ISBN 1-55297-693-9 (pbk.)
1. Mechanics – Vocational guidance 2. Occupations.
I. Title. II. Series
331.124162 21   HD8039.M43.L54   2003

Published in the United States in 2003 by
Firefly Books (U.S.) Inc.
P.O. Box 1338, Ellicott Station
Buffalo, New York, USA, 14205

National Library of Canada Cataloguing in Publication Data

Liebman, Daniel
          I want to be a Mechanic

ISBN 1-55297-695-5 (bound)
ISBN 1-55297-693-9 (pbk.)

1. Mechanics (Persons) – Juvenile literature.   I. Title

TJ157.L53 2003   j621.8'16'023'   C2002-903689-5

Published in Canada in 2003 by
Firefly Books Ltd.
3680 Victoria Park Avenue
Toronto, Ontario, Canada, M2H 3K1

Photo Credits

© AP Photo/Ed Andrieski, page 13
© AP Photo/Kevin Glackmeyer, page 21
© AP Photo/The Tennesseean, Randy Piland, page 8
© AP Photo/Waterloo Courier, Sarah Schutt, page 9, back cover
© Mark Dixon/BongoPhoto, pages 7, 22
© MediaFocus International, LLC, pages 12, 19, 20
© Francisco J. Rangel, front cover
© Stone/Michael Rosenfeld, pages 16-17
© Weststock, page 18
© George Walker/Firefly Books, pages 5, 6, 10-11, 14, 15, 23, 24

The author and publisher would like to thank:

Nash Garage Ltd., Toronto
Canadian Tire (Danforth Ave.), Toronto
Ideal Bike Inc. (Maggie Anderson), Toronto
Khan & Sons Garage, Toronto

Design by Interrobang Graphic Design Inc.
Printed and bound in Canada by Friesens, Altona, Manitoba

The Publisher acknowledges the financial support of the Government of Canada through the Book Publishing Industry Development Program for its publishing activities.

Machines have many parts. Mechanics work with different kinds of machines.

Mechanics make sure machines are running well.

They fix machines that need to be repaired.

Auto mechanics have to know how different makes and models work.

A mechanic helps keep a car safe to drive.

Sometimes, the mechanic needs to check underneath a car. This car is on a lift.

Mechanics enjoy working with their hands.

Good mechanics can find out a lot by using their eyes and ears.

There are different kinds of mechanics. Bicycle mechanics make sure your bike is safe to ride.

Trucks need mechanics. So do motorcycles, lawn mowers and tractors.

Mechanics use different tools for different jobs. Screwdrivers, pliers and power tools are all important.

A computer helps show where the problem is. Mechanics learn by going to school and working on the job.

Nothing is too small for this airplane mechanic to check.

Mechanics enjoy working together and learning from each other.

Safety is important for everyone! This mechanic is wearing goggles to protect his eyes.

The mechanic checks everything again to make sure the car is safe. Later, he will take it for a test drive.

The car is now ready. The mechanic explains the repairs. He makes sure the customer is happy.

It's a busy job! But mechanics always feel good when they know they have fixed the problem.